45 Day

Self-Improvement

Handbook

45 Daily Ideas, Habits, and Action-Plan for
Becoming More Productive, Persuasive,
Influential, Sociable and Self-Confident

A.V. Mendez

TABLE OF CONTENTS

The Daily Advantage (My Main Message)

I tend to write books with lots of "mini-topics" in them. The reason is that success in any endeavor, is the result of incremental improvements done and achieved daily and weekly. That's why most of my books are about small daily actions in everything that we do. It's not just about that one big thing. It's about 25, 40, or 70+ small ideas, that when combined together, brings in the best result imaginable.

Also, some of the things I write about aren't groundbreaking methods. They are mostly simple, easy-to-implement ideas that a lot of us **already know about but choose not to implement.**

My job is not to give you more information. If information is the key to success, then everyone with an internet connection will be more productive, self-confident, persuasive, emotionally healthy, physically fit and financially rich already. We are in the golden age of information and we can get almost any information we need just from a simple Google search.

My job is to give you a structure you can follow and present the information in a way that will maximize your intention and capacity to take action.

My job is to make everything as simple as possible for you so you don't quit from being overwhelmed.

My job is to show the importance of the ideas in this book so you'll have better incentives to do something about your problem.

This book will help you do all of that when it comes to your lack of self-confidence.

Free Gift

As a thank you for getting this book, I would like to give you the initial report that you can use if you're not ready to commit to a long-term challenge just yet.

It's a short report called "The 10-Day Self-Improvement Challenge."

The goal of that report is not to replace this book. The goal of the report is to help you get started.

To help you fight that initial reluctance to take action, you can start small and start with a 10-day challenge instead.

You can download your copy by going to this link below:

https://mailchi.mp/85b284031873/45day

Introduction

I have to hand it to you. Self-improvement can be hard at times. You could've easily just said, "you know what, I'm okay with being mediocre, at least I'm not tired." This may seem funny for some, but I've heard so many people say this before.

It's easier to just do nothing and stay the same. But you chose to improve as a person and that's something to be commended. With that said, it's not going to be easy. There are days when you'll just want to lay all day in your bed. There are days when it'll be tempting to just grab a handful of caffeine-filled drinks instead of drinking water.

But that's normal.

So you have to build a habit that will be the foundation of your success. And that's exactly what I am going to show you. Small ideas, that when added on top of each other, becomes a powerful agent of change.

4 Main Section

We are going to focus on 4 main aspects of self-improvement. Productivity, Influence, Self-Confidence and Social Skills.

Productivity.

Productivity is the ability to do work that matters. It's not just about getting things done. It's about doing things that you find important and doing it efficiently and effectively.

Influence.

Influence is the ability to affect other people's way of thinking and decisions.

Self-Confidence.

Self-Confidence, in simple term, is the ability to think that "you can do it."

Social Skills.

Social Skills is the ability to "connect" with other people (family, friends, strangers, colleagues, officemates, etc.)

We'll discuss this one by one at the start of every section.

Why You Should Start a 45 Day Self-Improvement Challenge (How to Use This Book)

Each small idea may seem trivial or simple. But trust me, improving in all of these 4 aspects every day, even for just a little bit, will have a positive ripple effect in your life.

That's why I created the 45-day self-improvement challenge. Each day, for the next 45 days, you can read one idea and then implement the action guide included in each chapter.

The reason I chose 45 days is because I found the usual 30-day challenge not as effective for me. The reason, I suspect, is because it takes me longer to adapt to a new habit than the average person. Studies show that you can build a habit in as few as 21 days. So I decided to double that number and just rounded it to 45 days, so it'll be at 1 ½ month of building a habit in the 4 main aspects of self-improvement. Now, self-improvement obviously shouldn't stop at 45 days. Self-improvement is a lifetime of commitment to get better. But starting something is better than starting nothing at all.

The 45-Day Challenge

The Challenge for Productivity (Day 1-10)

The Challenge for Persuasion and Influence (Day 11-20)

The Challenge for Self-Confidence (Day 21-33)

The Challenge for Your Social Skills (Day 34-45)

Each section consists of at least 10 days' worth of ideas (one each day). My hope is that you'll use the "mini ideas" every day so you can improve in each aspect of your self-improvement journey. Each idea is simple enough that most people can do them. Think of each idea as a Lego brick that you slowly build every day. In time, you'll see that you already built a house that can stand on its own.

Section 1 – The Challenge for Productivity

We are a generation of easily distracted people. Studies show that a goldfish has an even better focus than us. It's no wonder why we couldn't get things done!

Be honest with yourself here. How many times do you waste every day watching Netflix, browsing Instagram and other social media platforms?

I would guess that you waste at least 50% of your time every week (and that's being conservative). This isn't a knock on you. The majority of us waste our time on things that wouldn't bring us results. It has gotten so bad that countries like France are now banning e-mail and making any form of work connection illegal after office hours.

The goal of this section is simple:

To help you maximize your effectiveness & productivity, and help you avoid procrastination.

1 – Get Out of Your Own Head and Just Do

If there's one idea from this book that I wish everyone would implement, then this must be it. This is the greatest single secret of the most productive people in the world. It's not the apps, it's not the to-do list, it's not even the ability to focus (although it's definitely at the top).

It's the ability to get out of your own head and just do what you know you're supposed to be doing. This is obviously harder said than done. But it's the most important thing you can do in your quest for a more productive life.

Getting out of your own head means not trying to think too much about everything that you do. It's about the speed of implementation. Got an idea? If it's small enough and easy enough to do, then just try it immediately.

Do not get bogged down by the details. Just apply your idea fast. Fail fast if you must, at least you now have one less idea that you know doesn't work. That means you don't have to make the same mistake again in the future.

Action Guide:

1 – Do you have any small, easy-to-do ideas that you aren't putting into action? Maybe an article that you want to write? A sport you wanted to try? Or a band that you want to see? Productivity doesn't always have to be about work. It's about doing things that make you better. If you think watching your favorite band will make you feel awesome, thus making you more inspired at work, by all means, go buy that ticket today and attend that concert! Find that one small thing you can do today... and do it!

2 - The Art of Saying No

We're bombarded with request nowadays. Friend requests, meetings, "just a second of your time", and many more.

The problem lies in not really knowing how to say no. We're afraid that we'll sound rude and we're afraid that other people may start hating us.

But if you want to reclaim your time, then you have to start learning how to say no.

So how do you do it? The key is to respond in a respectful manner. In a way that doesn't make them feel bad for getting rejected. For example, if an officemate requested a meeting at your busiest time, then simply tell him this: "Hey John, 9am is my most productive time at work, do you mind if we do it later at 1pm instead?" If you're respectful and sincere, you are more likely to get a positive response.

Action Guide:

1 - We get tons of requests every day, say no to even just one of them. You don't necessarily have to

perfect the art of saying no, just choose one to say no to today. What we're doing is just practicing how to say no. If you've been a "Yes man" for most of your life, then this will be harder to do. So choose something easy to say no to. Maybe a lunch request, or someone wanting to borrow your pen (just make sure that you're actually about to use it). It doesn't matter how small or big that request is, the point is to know the feeling of saying the word "no."

3 - Time Chunking

Do you feel tired after every work-day? Do you feel like you've been in the office all day after an hour or two of work? I have the solution for you.

It's called Time-Chunking. It's a simple method of working in chunks of time. It could be 25 minutes, then 5 minutes of rest, then 40 minutes of work and then maybe 10 minutes of rest.

It's about focusing on one specific task per time-chunk. Let's say that you're a writer who wants to finish her novel. Your goal for the day is to finish 1 chapter and write 3,000 words.

What you can do is schedule 2 hours of writing time. You'll then chunk your time into 25-40 minutes of writing and 5-15 minutes of rest.

By following the time chunking method, you'll have a schedule that looks like this:

Writing [00:00 - 35:00]
Rest (Stretch, Play a Mobile Game) [35:00 - 45:00]
Writing [45:00 - 1:15]

Rest [1:15-1:30]
Writing [1:30 - 2:00]

As you work more hours, you become less productive and less focused, what you can do is to schedule more time for rest. This will help you tremendously in being more productive in your chosen task.

Action Guide:

1 - How can you apply the time-chunking method today? What is your most important task for the day? Apply the time-chunking method on task that takes more than 30 minutes to do.

Apply the time-chunking method and see the results for yourself. I'll bet you'll be amazed at how more productive you can be. You'll eventually use this method in pretty much all your tasks in the future.

4 - F**k Perfectionism

This is one of the leading cause of inactions. We think that in order for us to succeed, we must always be perfect in everything we do.

Nothing can be further from the truth, getting things done is better than not doing stuff in the first place.

In our search for perfection, we may forget to take action. We think that "if it's not perfect, then it shouldn't be done." This is the mindset that will destroy your chance of being productive.

In fact, I want you to delete the word "perfection" in your dictionary. There's no such thing as perfect. You are never going to achieve perfection. Unless you're a scientist, a NASA engineer or a doctor, or any job where life and death depends on you getting that thing perfect, then you don't have to aim for perfection.

Aim for progress instead. Aim for getting better every single day.

Action Guide:

1 - What are the things that you're putting off doing because you want those things to be perfect? What tasks are you not implementing simply because you're afraid that it's going to suck anyway? Start doing those things today. You have no excuse now, perfection is your enemy and progress is your friend. Remember that and you'll start to actually get more important things done.

5 - Does To-Do Lists Works?

Some experts will say that it works and some will say it doesn't. So who are we supposed to believe?

The answer is no one. Because most productivity tactics such as to-do lists are highly subjective. It's more about the person than the list itself.

Personally, I found them to be effective. Also, I make them as simple as possible. Doing this makes me want to actually do the tasks I'm supposed to be doing. Do not make it complicated, this will only make you feel anxious towards your to-do list.

4 Step Method

This is how I create my to-do list.

Step 1 - I write a list of the tasks that I need to do and I put as many as I can.

Step 2 - I choose only 5 that I must do today. If it can be done tomorrow (not urgent/not too important), then I'll put it on tomorrow's to-do list instead.

Step 3 - I prioritize the task that will have the biggest impact on my goals. For example, if you're a real-estate agent, then your most important goal is related to acquiring clients. So your #1 task for the day is something about talking to potential clients or advertising to get clients. Anything that has nothing to do with directly acquiring clients can be put in the last line of your to-do list.

Step 4 - Track the time it usually takes you to finish a specific task. Most of our daily tasks are repetitive. Track the minutes or hours required, so you can schedule the right amount of time it takes you to finish a task the next time you create your to-do list.

Action Guide:

1 - Create a "to-do list" for today or tomorrow's agenda. Follow the 4 step process outlined above.

6 - Your Environment

Your environment has a huge effect on your productivity.

Things like noise, lighting, and temperature can affect your motivation to do things even if you don't think it does. It's different for everybody, so you have to find that factor that really affects your productivity.

For me, it's the temperature. I like to work at 21 degrees Celsius to 25 degrees Celsius. That's 69.8 degrees Fahrenheit to 77 degree Fahrenheit for our Americans friends out there. If you work at home or you don't have anything to control the temperature with, get a fan and make sure that it's at a comfortable level.

When it comes to the noise, I prefer to work at maximum silence. Some people swear on working while blasting music on the background. That drives me crazy! But hey, everyone's different and that method may work for you so give it a try. You can also use noise-canceling headphones and play classical music or white noise. I found the white noise method to work well for me whenever I'm doing administrative tasks.

For creative tasks like writing or coming up with ideas, I use an earplug to block outside noise.

For lighting, there's no specific light source recommended to use. As long as you can see your keyboard when working, then you'll be just fine and it won't really have any effect on your productivity.

Action Guide:

1 - It's easy to go crazy about these things and really optimized your environment for more productivity. However, the advice I will give you is to make it as simple as possible. Just do one of the things I mentioned and see if it'll work for you. Don't do them all at once! You'll waste your time trying to come up with the perfect solution and you'll just end up pissed at yourself for wasting energy, on things you shouldn't really spending so much time on. I'm not saying these things aren't important, they are (that's why I wrote them), but don't over-optimized your way to better productivity. Just do one thing at a time and then add the next thing once you adequately implemented the first idea.

7 - Killing Online Distractions

Distractions are everywhere! Today, the biggest distraction that we have is online. Things like e-mail, Facebook, YouTube, and even Desktop applications ringing with notifications.

If possible, disconnect the internet while working. This idea may be impossible to some, but what you can do is to *schedule your distraction time* instead.

What I do is I set a schedule for mindless tasks like browsing Facebook, watching YouTube and doing other stuff that doesn't really help my productivity. By doing this, I effectively lessen my distractions while working. Now, I only have to fight the urge to get off my current task to browse crap online every once in a while (unlike before when I'm literally distracted every 5 minutes).

Action Guide:

1 - Schedule your "distraction time." Heck, add it to your to-do list if you must. For example, your to-do list could look like this.

8am-9am - work

9am - 9:10am - YouTube a.k.a. stupid stuff
9:10-10am - work ….

Sure, you're still technically not being productive by watching YouTube. But I would rather have 2 hours of productive time than be distracted by the thought of watching YouTube all day long.

8 - Process Maps

If you're serious about being the most productive you can be, then you have to start creating your own process maps. Process maps are written steps on how to achieve a specific task that you normally do every day.

Process maps are helpful because once you have a proven process, you can now use that plan to outsource a certain task and free up your time.

Even if you have no plans on outsourcing, you should still create one because it'll streamline the process and make things easier for you.

For example, I do SEO (search engine optimization) for other people. Instead of mindlessly doing the tasks needed every time a client comes in, I follow the process map I created instead.

Before, my process looked like this:

1 - Get a client
2 - Ask what my client wants me to do (which sometimes tends to be the things that wouldn't help their specific problems)

3 - Do the task they asked me to do

Now, my process looks like this:

1 - Get a client
2 - Let them fill-up the form regarding a specific type of service that they want me to do
3 - Find out if that's the specific service they need
4 - Accept or reject the client's request.
5 - Let them know the best solution for their problem instead.

This example is a little bit on a high-level stuff...

Let's bring it down to more of an "everyday" stuff you may encounter.

Let's talk about deleting large files you may not need anymore. Instead of letting a big file collect virtual dust, you can streamline the process by creating a process map.

Example:

A- Have you opened the file in the last 6 months?

B - If Yes, then you may still need it. Put it on an external hard drive instead.

C - If No, then you may not need the file anymore. Can you delete this file already?

D - Confirm if you might actually need it in the future. Ask your employees if you still need the file.

E - If Yes, then don't delete it but put them on an external hard drive instead.

F - If no, then delete the file.

Your process map will obviously differ based on your organization. Create one and then adjust accordingly as you learn more about yours.

Action Guide:

1 - What tasks are you doing every day that needs a process map? Create one for each and save it on a new folder called "Company Name Process Maps."

9- Nightly Preparation

Every day, I come to work ready to implement my plans from the day before. This makes *getting started* easier. This makes me less likely to wander off before I actually do something.

Every night, I prepare the tasks that I need to finish on the next day. If I have a writing session, I would open the Google Drive where my outline is and I would open Microsoft Word for the actual writing. In addition, I would close off tabs that doesn't relate to the act of writing. That means no Facebook, no YouTube, no sports articles… just my outline and my word file.

I would also put a bottle of water beside my laptop the night before. In addition, I'll also set up my Pomodoro timer clock on the right side of my desk. Now I have everything I need to write. No more distractions and all the tools are already there.

This gives me the best chance of actually getting started.

Try it, it somehow forces your brain to be on "action mode" instead of mindlessly wandering off the internet's black hole.

Action Guide:

1 - Prepare the tools that you need for tomorrow's task. Anything that you don't need shouldn't be on your desk. No phones, no pencils, no cellphone chargers, none of anything you don't absolutely need.

10 - Take Out the Trash

No, I don't mean the literal trash.

What I mean are the nagging personal issues you haven't taken care of. Maybe a tax bill, a ticket, or credit card bills that needs to be paid soon.

You can choose to ignore them but they won't go away. In fact, these little baby dragons of a problem may manifest into something bigger and *bite you in the behind* later. That tax bill can turn into a case against you in 6 months. That ticket may turn into jail time. Those credit card bills may turn into hundreds of thousands if you don't pay attention to it now.

Trust me, it'll be much better dealing with it now while these nagging problems are still at the beginning stages. Leave them be and they might make your life a living hell in the future. Sure, it's nice to just "forget about it." But that won't solve the problem, it'll only make things worse.

It's in your best interest to take out the trash now. Your future self will thank you for it.

Action Guide:

1 - What are the trash hiding in your closet? What are the consequences of keeping them in your room? Is it worth the future pain? Probably not. So make a list of "trash" you should take out and deal with it immediately.

Section 2 – The Challenge for Persuasion and Influence

In this section, we will focus on how you can affect other people's decision and response to certain things.

Influence is not about manipulation. It's about pointing someone on the right direction. If you use persuasion and influence in a negative manner, then you should be ashamed of yourself. However, using it for good is a noble idea and will bring good karma for you.

Imagine if you're selling life insurance and you really believe that your product can help young families. Wouldn't you think that it's your moral responsibility to persuade and influence them to buy the right financial plan for them?

In this case, you're using persuasion and influence for the better good of other people.

Persuasion and Influence is powerful, but you have to use it the right way.

11 - Ask

It baffles me how many people aren't willing to ask for something even though they really wanted to get the things that they desire.

The bible said, "Ask and you shall receive."

If you want a promotion, then ask.

If you want someone to buy what you're selling, then ask if they're interested in learning more about your product.

If you want to know how someone feels about you, then ask!

"But dude, it isn't that simple! What if I get rejected? What if I make a fool of myself?"

Well, rejection happens, and rejection sucks. But there's really no other way around it. I wish I could say that you'll get everything you asked for. But you won't. That's the bitter truth.

But I would rather be rejected that live with regrets of *what if.*

"What if I asked and my boss said yes for a promotion?"

"What if I ask her to marry me and she said yes?"

If the rewards far outweigh the failures, why wouldn't you consider asking?

Action Guide:

1 - Do you have something to sell? Or maybe something to ask of someone? Consider weighing the outcomes of a Yes and a No. Is it worth the risk? Most of the time, it is. So evaluate your situation and learn to ask for something you truly desire.

12 - Give

One of the greatest "trick" (if you can call it that) of persuasion and influence is called the Law of Reciprocity. It means that every time someone do something for us, we have this urge or more motivation to do or give something in return.

This is a proven fact; this isn't even a "probable study" anymore. People are just wired to give something back in return of a favor. It doesn't matter how big or small the act is.

If a friend gave us a free ride to work, we are more likely to say yes to a request that he'll ask of us to do in the future.

Obviously, you have to be reasonable. Just because you gave someone a free car ride doesn't mean he's going to give you a million dollars. However, small favors and reasonable requests are very likely to be accepted.

A warning though, do not use the law of reciprocity to manipulate other people. If your intention is to give because you want something in return, people will see that you're a fraud and the law of reciprocity will have a negative effect instead.

Action Guide:

1 - What can you offer that other people will find valuable? Maybe an eBook you wrote? An advice for a friend? A gift card you aren't using anymore? It doesn't have to be a material thing. It could be your words of wisdom and it could be your time. All of us each has our own value to offer the world. We just have to look closer and discover what it is.

13 - Become a Celebrity

Let's face it. Celebrities are one of the most influential group of people in the planet. Somehow, we're head over heels in pretty much anything they say and do.

Not all of us can be "Brad Pitt or Angelina Jolie" famous.

But what you can do is try to become a celebrity in your market.

Let's say that you work as a CEO Advisor.

You can build influence and be a "celebrity" in your tiny market by creating content via videos, talk-shows, podcasts and written articles about CEO advisory. You are mimicking what the celebrities are doing by being everywhere. Being the "celebrity CEO consultant" can lead to more clients, more authority and more influence which leads to more sales.

Action Guide:

1 - What can you start today that will help you build celebrity status in your business/market? Focus on

one aspect first. It could be YouTube videos (or Facebook videos), podcasts, Facebook live where you teach people anything related to your topic, and talk-show style videos where you interview a client or anyone related to your market.

14 - Teach

If you want to influence someone, then you also have to educate them about your topic. Authority comes from knowing what you're talking about.

It's easy to be an authority in Pokemon if you actually know things about the game. Imagine being an amazing Pokemon player/collector at 10 years old around dozens of other kids interested in playing the game. You'll be a god to them. Why? Because you know something that they don't. They will want to be beside you. They will want to be around you so they can get more Pokemon knowledge.

This is the power of teaching. Your job or business is irrelevant. Teaching works. It influences other people especially if you're genuine and you give great information.

Action Guide:

1 - What knowledge do you have that may serve other people? Look at your experience. The jobs that you had, the businesses you've started. Whatever those experiences are, there will always be some kind of lessons that you can teach others.

Are you good at relationships? Then teach a couple friend how to create a better relationship.

Are you good at writing? Then teach writing to other people.

The main thing here is to teach what you know. This builds trust, authority, and influence, thus it adds to your ability to persuade other people to take action.

15 - Cultivate a Legend

Cultivating a legend means controlling the narrative about yourself. You should only do this if you are genuine and honest about your intentions.

Let's say that you want to be a famous comedian and you really like talking about your race. Then you can tell jokes about your race and be "the guy" who talks about his race. Now, if you're super racist and you always go over the line, then this strategy would backfire. You have to really know a lot about your race in order to talk about it.

Another example: Let's say that you wanted to influence your employees to be more productive. One of the tactics that works is you can check-up on them randomly and watch how they work. You can cultivate a legend by actually doing that strategy and making everyone know that you are "that guy."

Now, if you're not that type of boss, then it probably won't be an effective method to influence them. They'll just fake their work because they know that you actually don't care. So you have to be genuine. You have to cultivate a real legend that people will know you for.

Action Guide:

1 - Make a list of who you want your market to know you for and what you can do to cultivate it.

For example, let's say that you work as a non-fiction writing coach and you want them to know that you are a no-nonsense coach who can teach someone to write a book in 7 days or less.

Goal: To be a no-nonsense coach whom people recognize as someone who can teach other people to write a book in 7 days.

Things you can do to cultivate this legend:

1 - Teach the strategy behind writing fast

2 - Show testimonials of other people who have successfully written their books in 7 days or less

3 - Show books you've written in 7 days

4 - Vlog about the process of writing a book fast

Doing and showing these things cultivate the legend that you are the "no-nonsense, quick writing" coach.

16 - WIIFM?

Oftentimes, when we're trying to persuade or influence someone, we tend to focus on what we can offer. But we also have to think about what they really want.

"WIIFM - What's in it for me?"

"Why should I listen to you?"

"Why should I take the time to watch your sales video?"

You have to tell the reasons why they should choose you instead of every other consultant out there.

You have to give them a product benefit that can solve his problems.

If you're selling a house, you have to show them how this house can make them happy, how it can help their kids in various aspects of their lives as they grew up. You have to attached your product to an emotional benefit.

What's in it for the customer or client?

Find out what it is and tell them about it.

Action Guide:

1 - Look at your last rejection. Whether in business, your job, your relationship or your craft. Look back at your last rejection and ask if you gave them enough reasons to say yes to your request. Did you give them the main benefits of the product? Did you ask what the market really wants?

Write the answers down on a piece of paper and write what you can do next time to avoid the same rejection.

17 - Show Energy

Showing energy doesn't mean you're always speaking loudly and being animated. It's an art form in itself. It's about the way you talk, the way you use your body and the way you use your voice.

People like to communicate with someone who's very aware of the situation.

If he's in a happy setting, he will be more animated. He will speak a little louder than usual and he will smile more.

On the other hand, if he's on a sad setting, he'll know when to shut up and when to speak. He'll know the tone of his voice and he'll know how loud or how soft he should speak.

This is what we call "controlled energy."

It's about knowing how to react on a certain environment and situation.

Action Guide:

1 - The way you act on a specific situation matters. Sometimes, these actions will be pretty obvious.

For some, they will still wonder why everything got awkward on a funeral, where they made an inappropriate joke at an inappropriate time.

So just be aware of situations you are in and act accordingly. Don't just show energy, show the right energy.

18 - Awareness of Your Own Feelings

Sometimes, our feelings can get the best of us. Someone will say something rude and we'll snap. Someone will do something stupid and we'll go *batshit* crazy. Sure, we may be justified to act that way but that is not how you create influence.

People like to follow someone they can emulate. They like their role models to be perfect. This is an impossible standard, so we shouldn't strive for perfection.

What we should strive for is progress. We should strive for learning.

One of the things we should have is an awareness of our own feelings.

When you're feeling like you are about to snap at someone, immediately acknowledge that feeling. "I'm mad and I want to punch this guy." Next, breath in and out 3 times. Do it slowly and count 1 2 3, 3 2 1 each cycle. This will make you calmer. By this time, you are now less likely to snap since you now have a grasp on your emotion.

You can still add the next step which is about the alternative action. Think about the things you can do instead. You can walk away, you can calmly talk to the person, or you can do the initial reaction you had. But before you make a decision, make sure that you know the consequences of your action.

Action Guide:

1 - Practice having awareness of your own feelings. Whenever you're in some kind of situation, acknowledge the feeling that you have and breath in & out 3 times. Manage your emotions well so you won't regret the consequences of your actions later.

19 - The Power of Body Language

They say that less than half of our communication are words.

The other half (and more) is body language.

Body language is the way you look at someone, the way you stand, what your hand does and many other factors.

People are attracted to people who are confident and assured.

The worst things you can do are:

-To fidget in front of your conversation partner.

-To overly move your hands while talking.

-To put your hands behind your back or your pocket. It should be on the side or being animated a little when the words you're saying requires it.

-To hunch forward. You should stand straight with your shoulders back.

-To never look at the person you're talking to. You should be having eye contact at least 50% of the time.

-To never smile, ever or when the situation requires it.

Follow these simple tips and you'll be 2x better than other people when it comes to having a conversation.

Action Guide:

1 - Choose one tip you can apply in your next conversation. Don't do them all at once if you're not a natural with any of them. Just choose one so you won't overthink about the actions. Thinking about what you're doing while you're doing it can be awkward. So practice it with someone you trust first. And then you can move on to strangers/customers/ clients once you found your groove.

20 - The Power of Vocal Tonality

Your vocal tone is part of the story. It is part of the conversation.

Imagine talking to someone about Disneyland and they talk like someone who's like a person whose dog recently died. That would be a depressing conversation.

Vocal tonality is about the speed and the sound of your voice.

Is it slow and loud? Is it fast and quiet?

These affects how people listen to you.

If you want to make a point and you want people to listen to every word you say, then you must speak softly and speak a little slower than usual.

For example, let's say you are trying to make a point about the importance of vaccination. Then you'll say something like this:

"The most important thing is that you should bring your kids to the doctor within 1 week of birth"

Here's how this would play out:

"The most important thing is" - *You speak on a normal pace.*

"that you should bring your kids to the doctor within 1 week of birth" - *You speak slower and softer (so people will listen attentively)*

Vocal tonality affects how other people listen to you. And as you know, when people listen, they are more likely to be influenced by you.

Action Guide:

Practice conversations in front of the mirror. Don't be afraid to look and sound stupid. You are not recording so nobody is going to watch or listen to it. But hey, if you want to record and see your progress, by all means, record away.

Section 3 – The Challenge for Self-Confidence

Self-confidence is NOT about knowing that you can do everything. The truth is, well, you can't.

Self-confidence is about having **the ability to recognize what you are capable of**. It's about having a belief in yourself based on what the evidence suggests.

Often, we conflate ego with self-confidence.

We admire guys like Kanye West. We say things like "Kanye West has lots of ego and he's successful." But no, Kanye West is successful because he has talent. And you know what, I feel like he would've been even bigger if not for his ego.

So don't mistake ego with self-confidence.

Self-confidence is better. It does not boast; it does not take pride.

Self-confidence is the foundation of one's belief in himself/herself.

21 – Acknowledge the Truth

Do not lie to yourself. This will only make things worse for you. If you're not achieving your goals and you feel bad about yourself, then start acknowledging how you feel and get a hold of the situation. This is not the time for avoiding the truth. This is the time to be honest and look at what place you're currently at. Will it be hard for you to accept that things haven't worked out so far? For sure. But as they say, "the truth will set you free."

Lying about your situation means you'll just waste more time contemplating and sobbing instead of using that time to pivot and get better.

So acknowledge the truth. Accept it and embrace it.

That is the first step to gaining confidence, and it can be liberating.

Action Guide:

1 – What are the hard truths that you need to accept in your life? Answer this question truthfully!

22 - Owning Your Stuff

You know what's one of the best ways to become unequivocally confident?

BE ACTUALLY GREAT AT WHAT YOU DO.

I know, mind-blowing stuff right! Sarcasm aside…You have to be good at what you do because it's going to be the foundation of your confidence. When you're good at what you do, you doubt yourself less. You become less prone to self-criticism. You work on your weaknesses instead of blaming yourself for your mistakes.

Being good means being aware of your current skills or knowledge level in your own field, and then deliberately working on yourself to improve every single day.

Kobe Bryant never stopped practicing. Stephen King kept on writing.

These guys kept on improving every single day.

Action Guide:

1 - What is the main skill that you have? Start taking deliberate actions to help you improve this specific skill. If it's sports, then schedule a daily practice. If it's writing, then go write every day. If it's in the academia, then go read every single moment that you can. Never stop learning and never stop improving. That's how you achieve greatness and true confidence.

23 - Look at Your Track Record

Another way to be confident is to look at your track record. Look at what the evidence suggest that you can use to justify being confident about yourself.

So many of us undervalue our own experiences. "Oh, I'm just an entry level employee", "oh I've only worked here for 3 years so *10yearsMatt* is better than me."

Don't undervalue your experience. Look at the things you've done no matter how little your experience is. Everybody starts small. The achievement doesn't have to be mind-blowing either. You don't have to compare yourself to other people to do this thinking exercise.

Action Guide:

1 – Look back at your experiences and think of all the "mini achievements" that you've done. I promise you that you will find lots of small things to be proud of. It could be an award from your team leader. It could be a process that you create for your team. It could be a 2nd place trophy. It could be anything related to your skill.

Make a list and name it "My Confidence Foundation." Try to come up with at least 10 and read it every week for additional motivation. This is true confidence, backed by proof that you can actually do something awesome.

24 - Eliminate Your Ego

As I told you in the beginning of this chapter, your ego is different from your self-confidence. Self-confidence is real. Ego is destructive.

Ego is the voice that says you're better than everybody, even though you're really not. Ego is the voice that says you can have everything even though your current action doesn't support that kind of thinking. Ego is the voice that says "f*ck everybody! It's me against the world."

Don't let yourself be consumed by this voice.

It may feel good at first. But it'll eventually lead you to a crash!

The ego says you're too good to hang out with your old friends anymore… Develop this kind of thinking and The Universe, God or whatever force you want to call it will bring you back down to the ground.

The ego said "I'm the Best Ever" even though the evidence suggests otherwise.

Let others praise you from what you've already done, not what you are yet or about to do.

Action Guide:

1 – Notice when the ego is creeping in. Notice when you feel moral superiority against others.

Stay humble, keep your head down and just do the work. If you're good, then people will notice. Don't mistake being the best as the man who shouts the loudest.

25 - Ask Good Questions

Asking good questions is one of the foundational piece of having conversation with other people. So how does this translate into self-confidence?

When you ask good questions, people respond to you in a positive manner. You get to build "social points" for being a good conversationalist. People are attracted to you because you know how to talk to them. People starts to like you because you know how to steer a conversation by asking the right questions. People will like you because you keep making them talk about themselves.

So learn to ask good questions and learn to ask the right questions.

Good questions are most often about the person you're talking to.

So ask questions based on their interests, their job, and their achievements.

You not only help their self-esteem; you also help yours!

This is a win-win situation for the both of you.

Action Guide:

1 – Think of some questions you can ask a friend to help his or her self-esteem. These questions will differ based on their situation.

Some examples are:

A – *What's it like to be promoted?*

B – *You seem to enjoy your job. Can you give me some advice on how I can do the same?*

C – *You're really good at what you do, what's your schedule like?*

26 - Manage Your Highs and Lows

There are times when you would feel like you're on top of the world. And then there are times when you would feel like you're on the lowest of the lows.

Your ability to manage your highs and lows will determine whether you will become successful or not. So here's a truth bomb for you. Accept now that some shitty things may happen to you. Accept now that failure is going to be part of the process. If you're building something good for yourself, then it must be hard, and the harder it is, the more likely you are to experience some failure along the way.

But failing doesn't have to mean that you lost. The good news is life almost always give us a second chance, a third chance, a fourth, and so on.

If you get some wins, go ahead and celebrate. But then go back to work after a little bit of celebration.

If you get some losses, go cry if you must. Eat your ice cream to make yourself feel good. Then go back to the drawing board and make a list of lessons you learned from that loss. Then put your head down and get back to work.

Action Guide:

1 – Celebrate all your wins by giving yourself some kind of reward for a job well done. Don't overdo it! The type of win you have should match your reward. Got a promotion? Get that guitar you've been dreaming of, not the new BMW. Deal with losses by acknowledging your pain and then start working out the solution to your problems.

27 - Personal Hygiene

Having a clean physical appearance is already proven to help us be more confident.

Imagine being in the office and smelling like you haven't had a nice bath in weeks. Everybody will turn away from you and you'll be laughed at behind your back. Uhm, not a good feeling to have.

So take care of yourself. Spend a little if you must.

The basics are your hair, your face, your body, your nails, and your teeth.

Most of these should be taken care of on a daily or weekly basis.

Action Guide:

1 – Take care of your personal hygiene by doing the following:

A – Cut your hair every 3-4 weeks. Find the best haircut for your own head shape. It's not just about how long or how short your hair is. It's about having the right cut for the shape of your face.

B – Wash your face twice a day, preferably once in the morning and once before you sleep.

C – Use a soap that makes you smell good or use a light perfume on your body. Also, always use a deodorant no matter where you are going.

D – Cut your nails at least once a week.

E – Brush your teeth for 5 minutes 2-3 times a day. Use an electric toothbrush if you can.

28 - Dress to Impress

Whether we like it or not, people will always judge a book by its cover. Also, people will always have a stereotype of who we are just by looking at our clothes.

My advice is to wear something based on the occasion.

If you're at work, and it's very professional there, then use a tailored suit. It doesn't have to be mega expensive. The key to dressing well is the fit. The materials used is also important but the fit is what will determine whether you look good on a suit or not.

If you're in a business conference, don't try to be cool and wear shorts. First of all, you're a d*ck if you do that. Second of all, you're not going to be taken seriously by potential business partners.

So dress according to the occasion.

This will boost your confidence a lot. It's been proven that wearing a nice fitting suit or dress makes you feel good about yourself. It's not always cheap but the right pair of suit is always worth the price.

1 – Go watch YouTube videos on what to wear during certain occasions. Dressing well can easily double your confidence as long as it is the right fit. The right dress will make you feel like a King or a Queen.

29 - Momentum Builder

One of the most underrated confidence-builder is momentum.

When you feel like the momentum is on your side, keep going and don't stop working! When it feels like everything you touch turns into gold, the keep on reaching!

This is not the time to stop and reflect. This is the time to take action.

Trust me, momentum can shift fast. So use it to your advantage.

Momentum seems to work not just in the physical aspect of the word, but also in our actions. Stuff like writing every day, selling your products, or winning sports games. Momentum is powerful and it can build your confidence fast. Just ride the wave and keep working.

Action Guide:

1 – Notice when you're having a momentum in what you're doing. Did you get a 4 game winning streak?

Great, keep doing the same thing that helped you win 4 straight games. Don't change strategy. Don't overthink things and just follow the momentum.

30 - Surround Yourself with Good People

"You are the average of the 5 people you hang out with"

We all heard this before. In fact, this has become a cliché that people do not seem to value its importance anymore.

But there's a reason why it has become a cliché. Because it's true.

If you want to be successful, and all your friends does every Friday night is party, then hanging out with them won't help you achieve your goals.

When I say "surround yourself with good people," I don't just mean good in a moral sense of the word. I mean good as in "I'm working on improving myself too" sense of the word.

Find the right people and hang-out with them. Eventually, you'll notice your own improvement just by hanging out with the right people, who also have the same goals as you.

Action Guide:

1 – As hard as it is to do, you have to cut off some people in your lives. Cutting off people doesn't mean you stop being friends with them. It only means that you have to spend less time and energy with them. It's hard to be a successful basketball player if all your friends are alcoholic. It's impossible to become a good employee if all your friends hate their jobs.

Start making new friends that you know are going to make you better. Attend a seminar to meet some like-minded people, attend a boot camp to meet other people who wants to improve themselves. Go find where they hang out, make friends and keep lifting each other up.

31 - Face Your Fears

Facing your fears may be nerve-racking.

But it has so many benefits that your life will change just by facing each fear with an open mind. So many of us never face our fears because we're afraid of failures.

We justify it to ourselves by saying "If I never try, I'll never fail at it," but the truth is you already failed by not trying in the first place. You already failed because you didn't become who you are supposed to be.

So how do you face your fears?

You start with your smallest fears. You start with fears that doesn't have a big impact in your life.

Let's say one of your fears is talking to a cashier (yes, this condition exists).

Create a plan on how you can approach a cashier without being awkward.
Maybe on your first attempt, you just give your order and then smile a little bit at the cashier. Then you go

find another store… this time, you'll then talk to the cashier (maybe ask for some item), then smile and say thank you.

The point is to make it a process. Make the commitment small enough that you can do it easily.

Remember, Rome wasn't built in a day.

Action Guide:

1 – What are your fears? Make a list and start facing the smallest one you know you can beat! This will help you get a much needed confidence boost.

32 - Set a Small Target

The more you achieve, the more you build your self-confidence. That's why I recommend starting out by setting small targets. I know that every guru you see nowadays always say "Think Big! The sky is the limit!" Setting small targets doesn't mean you're thinking small. It just means you're thinking long-term. You're thinking about improving along the process as your targets gets bigger and bigger.

There's nothing wrong with starting small. Remember the consistent small wins leads to long-term big wins. Success is only a combination of small things done consistently.

Set small targets. These tiny successes will lead you to your breakthrough, thus giving you more confidence to go for the bigger fishes in the sea.

Action Guide:

1 – What is one small thing you can do every day that will directly lead you to your goal? Do it consistently and adjust to what works as you go along the process.

33 - Set a Big Target, Then Go Small

Once you start hitting small targets, now it's time to go big.

Hitting those small wins every day means you've already proven to yourself that you have what it takes. Those small wins are the proof that yes, your confidence is based on your skills and not just your ego.

The irony about big goals is that they're actually just a combination of different small goals roll into one.

Let's say that your goal is to lose 100lbs in 1 year. That is a big goal. Before, your goal maybe is to lose 8 lbs. That's easy to achieve, 100 in a year is hard.

That's why we will apply math into the goal.

100lbs in a year means you have to lose an average of 8.33 lbs. per month.

That's an average of 2.1 lbs. per week.

The next step is to focus on the daily actions that will lead you to losing 2.1 lbs. per week. These are things like your daily exercise, your gym time, and the food you eat.

By now, your end goal is to lose 100 lbs., but your process focuses on the daily things that you have to do in order to achieve your weekly shred of 2.1 lbs.

This is how you achieve a goal. This is how you build momentum and confidence.

Start small, go big, then go small again.

Action Guide:

1 – Set your big goal today. Then ask yourself, what are the weekly goals you should hit in order to achieve the long-term goal? Apply math in solving that problem if possible (see example above).

Section 4 – The Challenge for Your Social Skills

I used to be an extroverted person. But working from home for 4 years now somehow changed me into an introvert.

I prefer to work alone and I never seemed to enjoy talking to strangers (I used to feel awkward).

Then I got into sales and I learned to adjust. I realized that learning how to communicate well with friends, family, clients/customers are skills that we need to have in order to become more effective in what we do.

Social skills are as important as any of the topics we discussed in the past chapters.

Social skills help us become less awkward and more confident in our conversations.

Social skills make us better salespeople.

Social skills help us make a connection with our friends and family.

Social skills help us climb the corporate ladder.

Social skills help us connect with the best of the best in our field.

In this section, I will help you build your social skills one small idea and one tiny step at a time.

34 - The Right People

First things first. Your social skills are useless if you aren't using it with the right people!

So the first thing you should know is your goal.

Why do you want to get better at talking to people? Why do you want to learn how to communicate well?

Maybe you want to get a job, maybe you want to sell more cars this year, or maybe you want to sell your art.

Your reason will dictate who your main "audience" will be.

You will obviously be using your social skills with other people that has nothing to do with your goals (talking to your Starbucks barista), but you have to know who your main audience is because how you communicate with one set of market may differ from another.

The right people are the ones that will bring you closer to your goals.

Action Guide:

1 - Who are the right people for you? It could be your customers or clients. It could be listeners for your music. You have to know who they are and then you have to understand what makes them tick.

Exercise:

Define a goal that you want to achieve, then find out who the main audience will be. What is their motivation? What do they want to get out of their conversations? Why are they trying to connect with you?

Different motivations require different set of actions. Define yours.

35 - The Right Words

Every set of market will always have their own "insider terms." These are the terms that are being used in their inner circle.

If you don't know about these terms, then there's no way you will be able to connect with them.

Let's say that you are an internet marketer…

Then you must know words like: squeeze page, landing page, SEO, click through rate and all that mumbo jumbo. These are normal terms in their world.

How will you be able to connect with them if you have no idea what these terms means?

Knowing the right words means that you are "in" the group. It means that you are part of the tribe.

When you don't know the market's language, then It will feel like being in a foreign country. You'll feel lost because you won't understand what they're saying.

But the moment you learn (and they realize that you know) how to speak their language, you instantly become part of the ecosystem. You can now socialize and now have the ability to connect.

Action Guide:

1 - Study the "insider terms" of your market and know exactly what these words mean. In addition, learn how to use them in conversations. It's not enough that you know what it means. You also have to know what it does and its importance in the market.

36 - The Right Body Language

Your body language speaks volume about what you're conveying. Sometimes, your words may say one thing but your body language will show another.

The most important ones to know are eye contact, hand gestures, and posture.

For eye contact, it's always a good idea to follow the 50% rule. Look in the eyes of the person you're talking to 50% of the time. Staring at her for the entire conversation is just plain creepy!

For the hand gestures, put your hand on the side 50% of the time and then use your hand when you're discussing something a little bit more interesting.

For the posture, stand up straight/sit up straight with your shoulders back. When you're trying to show that you're interested and listening attentively, move your head a little bit forward to the direction of your conversation partner.

These are the basics that will help you get started in improving your social skills via body language.

Action Guide:

1 - Choose one body language and start applying it on your next conversation. You will feel awkward in the beginning because you're going to think about what you're doing. So relax and listen to your friend attentively. Once you've done this enough, it'll start to feel more natural to you and you'll immediately see the benefits of getting your body language on point.

37 - Acknowledging a Peer

Acknowledging someone means you'll make them realize that their presence is important. It means that you notice them and you noticed what they've done.

What they've done doesn't have to be a big deal either for you to notice it. Let's say that you see someone with a new dress, just mention how you like her dress and how it fits her well. Say as if it's just a passing remark. You don't have to make a big deal out of it. When someone gets something right on the job, a simple "great job on the X account" will mean the world to the other person.

Be generous on your acknowledgement and praise. You have no idea how much this can uplift other people's day. It doesn't cost you anything to do and it's one of the best ways to start being a trusted peer or friend.

Action Guide:

1 - Acknowledge someone today. Then do it again tomorrow.

38 - Downplay Their Mistakes

Telling someone that they're wrong and stupid is the fastest way to make an enemy. Sure, they may be on the wrong but that doesn't mean you should shout about it at the rooftops.

They already feel bad for making a mistake, you repeating that to their face won't solve anything.

Instead, what you can do is downplay their mistakes, and then mention how everybody (even you) can make mistakes regarding this certain project/incident. Next, give them a solution so they can avoid making the same mistake in the future.

For example, let's say that your friend Emmy bought the wrong cake for your friend's birthday party. Instead of saying how dumb she is, make her feel like it's not her fault because anyone could've made the same mistake.

Say something like:

"Emmy, don't worry about it. We've all been so stressed out lately that anyone could have bought the wrong cake. It looks the same as the one we wanted to buy so it's not really your fault. Why don't we go back to the shop and replace it?"

Doing this instead will make Emmy feel better and she will start to trust you more. Emmy will never forget this because this isn't a normal response most people are expecting.

Action Guide:

1 - When was the last time you made someone feel wrong and a little humiliated? Think about what you could have said and done in that situation. Write it down on a piece of paper and then make a list of the lessons you learned from that encounter.

39 - Listen

Why are we created with two ears and one mouth? Maybe because we are born to listen more than we speak!

In my conversations, I make sure that I speak at least only 40% of the time. Listening is the gateway to understanding someone. If you're only half-listening and thinking about other things while he's saying something, then you wouldn't fully understand his side.

Listening is a skill that I feel like has lost its appeal today. Everybody wants to be *the influencer.* We are in a world full of people who won't stop talking.

With that said, now is the perfect time to be a good listener. The world needs someone who can speak less and listen more. Someone who will understand our pains, our problems, and our desires.

When you start to listen more, you'll notice that people will easily trust you more, and give you details about their life that they won't reveal to other people.

The key to having better listening skills is not a hearing aid. It's your ability to focus and be genuinely interested in what they have to say.

Action Guide:

1 - On your next conversation, do not think about what you have to say to the person. Do not try to impress her with what you know. Just listen and try to understand how they feel about the topics you guys are discussing. Not missing any details about what they're discussing means you'll understand them more, thus making you someone who can relate to them on a deeper level.

40 - Take Notes

OK, I don't mean take notes while you're having the conversation. Take notes when you get home. What are the things that you did right in that last conversation? What are the things that you could've said or done better?

Take note of those lessons so you can be a better conversationalist.

When you're taking notes, always keep an open mind and don't kick yourself for making a mistake. This is not the time to doubt yourself. This is the time to learn how to use your experience and turn it into a lesson you can implement later.

In addition, taking notes isn't just about learning about you. It's also for learning about the other person. What do they want? What topics did they keep coming back to? Why are they talking to you in the first place?

Knowing the other party means you'll get to serve them more.

Action Guide:

1 - Buy a notebook and use it as your "conversation notes."
Start with your last conversation. What are the lessons you learned from that conversation? What are the things you did well and the things that you could have done better? Write them all down and review those notes at least once a week for the next 30 days.

41 - Encourage Other People

Most of us are insecure. We just can't help it. Advertising says that we should drive this car, then wear that brand and then own a certain house. But the truth is we don't really need all these things.

That's the reason why a lot of us are insecure people with low self-esteem.

You can become someone they can trust by being someone who will encourage them to "go for it."

It's nice to be the voice of positivity in a world full of pessimism.

For example, if a friend of yours feel insecure about their average performance this month, simply tell her that she can do better next month *for sure!* Tell her that she's capable of so much more, and she just have to focus on her goal of becoming a better employee.

You can also encourage someone by simply supporting whatever it is they want to achieve. Say you have an officemate who wants to learn how to play the guitar. Ask yourself, *how can you support him in learning the guitar?* You can buy him a guitar (which may seem overdone) or you can just buy him a $5 book about learning how to play the guitar. If you want to become a trusted peer in the office, then you have to support their interests outside of work as well.

The key is to be genuine in helping others. Don't ask for anything in return and make them feel that you are as invested to their success as they are to themselves.

Action Guide:

1 - Do you know somebody who needs more encouragement in their lives? Go on and make your move. Let them know that you support them and that you like them to "go for it." Make them realize that what they're trying to achieve is possible, and that you have no doubt that they can do it.

42 - Say Their Name

The sweetest sound we can hear will always be our own name. Every time someone mentions your name, you'll automatically turn to the person who said it. It's almost impossible to resist the temptation to look even if the word came out of an unfamiliar voice.

Mention someone's name often.

Use it on emails, conversation, stories, phone calls, text and Facebook messenger.

This simple idea alone can make them trust you faster.

Also, make sure that you are using the correct spelling and the correct pronunciation of their name. If you get it wrong, it'll have a negative effect instead.

Action Guide:

1 - Use someone's name in your conversation today. Preferably, choose someone whom you are still not too close with yet.

43 - No Bragging

Nobody likes a bragger.

A bragger instantly gets laughed at or talked about once he leaves the conversation.

You don't have to brag about your achievements. You don't have to brag about your branded clothes, your new car, or your *new anything*.

High-quality people (which you want to attract) are usually not impress with any of these things I mentioned above.

They are impress with values, stories, character and whatever cool thing you're doing for other people. The keyword here is OTHER people. If you talk about what you are offering other people (especially if it's something that is making their lives better), then you will impress the other person.

So don't brag about yourself. Trust me, you're not impressing someone of quality if all you talk about is how awesome you are.

Action Guide:

1 - Stop bragging and start helping.

What can you offer the other party that they may find valuable?

They don't care about what you have, they only care about what they can get from the relationship or the conversation.

44 - Introverts' Can Speak Too

Just because you consider yourself an introvert doesn't mean you shouldn't speak ever. Even if you are an introvert, there are times when you will be required to push yourself and become a good conversationalist. Sometimes, our jobs will require us to do something we are uncomfortable with.

I consider myself an introvert. But I decided to go into sales because I know that it is going to make me a better conversationalist. I know that the sales job that I have will push me to become better at understanding other people's wants and needs.

I know that it'll be harder for us introverts to speak our minds, but trust me, if you push through it, if you intentionally try to get better, then the rewards will be worth it.

Action Guide:

1 - Take some trainings, read some books, or hire a coach, so you can push through the uncomfortable phase of learning to have better social skills. The benefits of learning how to connect with other people are priceless.

45 - The Magic of Saying Thank You

It's a simple word.

It's easy to say and it only takes you 2 seconds to say the word – Thank You.

Then why aren't we saying this enough? Why are we always in a hurry? Why do we act as if we don't see the person in front of us?

A simple *thank you* can brighten up someone's day.

A simple *thank you* will add value (no matter how small that is) to someone's life.

So the next time someone say or did something nice to you, just say the words *thank you*.

And you know what's even better to do?

Look at the other person, say thank you and then smile.

It's not that hard to do and it'll make you feel better at the same time.

There's something about gratitude that makes our brain light up. Whenever we're thankful, our brain secretes a chemical called dopamine. This is the same chemical correlated with pleasure and reward. So the more grateful you are, the happier you become.

In addition, being a *gratitude monster* makes you likeable. It's not that hard to like someone who has a positive vibe.

Gratitude gives you this vibe!

Action Guide:

1 - Say the word "thank you" whenever possible. It doesn't matter how small or big the act is. Just look the person in the eye, say thank you, smile, and leave.

Bonus: Physical Fitness & Energy

Another aspect that we often forget when we're trying to improve ourselves is the physical fitness part of our lives.

I suspect that the reason is because we think that it's too hard to improve physically. We have this notion that we need to lose lots of weight and gain pure muscle mass to be healthy. And doing these things are hard … so we just ignore it.

The truth is you don't have to look like Rocky or The Terminator…. You just have to be fit enough so you can maximize your energy and do the things that you want to do.

My advice is simple, because honestly, I don't go crazy with my own physical fitness routine.

Every day, I just go for a walk (20-30 minutes) and stretch. I drink at least 8 glasses of water just like what the doctors said and I try not to eat any carbohydrates after 6pm.

That's it. In this aspect of my life, I'm just getting started in making myself better so I don't go crazy with it. I just start with those habits and then I'll add more in the near future.

The last thing that you want to do is overwhelm yourself with impossible goals and tasks. There's a reason why this book is structured that way. It's because I don't want you to get information overload. I want you to choose some ideas that you like and implement them in your life one day at a time.

I follow the same principle in almost everything I do. I start small and then I add some ideas/habits/ practices as the day goes by. It's that simple, and I'm confident that it'll work for you too.

Conclusion

Improving yourself is hard, but it can be simple. Our own success is just a combination of little things done right consistently. You start with one idea and then you add another one, and then you repeat the process over and over again, which then leads you to better results in every aspect of your life.

The stonecutter's credo always reminds me to be persistent:

"When nothing seems to help, I go and look at a stonecutter hammering away at his rock perhaps a hundred times without as much as a crack showing in it. Yet at the hundred and first blow, it will split in two, and I know it was not that blow that did it, but all that had gone before." *Jacob Riis*

It's not about that one big blow. It's about hammering away, little by little until you see the cracks finally showing. And just like the stonecutter's credo said, you'll know exactly which blow did it.

I wish you all the best and I hope this book served you well.

I Need Your Help

If you enjoyed reading this action-packed, daily guide, I would like to request for you to leave a short book review on Amazon.

I understand that reviewing a book takes some of your time and I want you to know that I really appreciate you as a reader.

I treat each review as precious and I would really appreciate you taking the time of your day to leave one on the book's Amazon page.

Thanks for reading this book and I will see you on the next one.

OTHER BOOKS:

Check out more self-improvement books here:

https://www.amazon.com/A-V-Mendez/e/
B00XU2UW5S

I have books for self-confidence, self-esteem,
building your socials and people skills, and many
more!

www.ingramcontent.com/pod-product-compliance
Lightning Source LLC
Chambersburg PA
CBHW031353060726
47590CB00007B/2758